SEE & EXPLORE
LIBRARY

DINOSAURS

·AND·HOW·THEY·

·LIVED·

Written by
Steve Parker

Editorial consultant
William Lindsay
British Museum (Natural History)

Illustrated by
**Guiliano Fornari
Sergio**

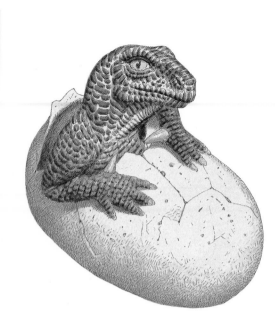

A DK PUBLISHING BOOK

Editor Angela Wilkes
Art editor Roger Priddy

Editorial director Jackie Douglas
Art Director Roger Bristow

First American Edition, 1991

10 9 8

Published in the United States by
DK Publishing, Inc., 95 Madison Avenue,
New York, New York 10016

Copyright © 1991 Dorling Kindersley
Limited, London

Visit us on the World Wide Web at
http://www.dk.com

ISBN 1-879431-13-0
ISBN 1-879431-28-9 (lib.bdg.)

Library of Congress Catalog Card Number 91-060143

Phototypeset by SX Composing, Essex
Reproduced in Singapore by Colourscan
Printed in Spain by Artes Graficas, Toledo S.A.

D.L.TO: 953-1996

CONTENTS

WHAT WERE THE DINOSAURS?

Picture a dinosaur in your mind. It may be quite big and fierce, with long legs and sharp teeth. Or it may have stumpy legs, a long neck and tail, a tiny head, and a body as big as a bus. All of us have our own idea of what a dinosaur looked like.

But what does the word *dinosaur* mean? It was invented by an English scientist, Richard Owen, in 1841. At that time many large fossil bones were being discovered. Owen decided that the creatures the bones came from were not a type of lizard, as some people suggested. He invented a new name for them – *Dinosauria*, meaning "terrible lizards."

What exactly are dinosaurs? They are animals – or rather they *were*, since the last of them died out about 65 million years ago. During the millions of years of the Earth's history many kinds of animals came and went. The dinosaurs were among them.

Giant reptiles

There were many kinds of dinosaurs, but they were all reptiles, just as turtles, lizards, and snakes are. They had scaly or leathery skin, lungs, and young that hatched from eggs with shells. Not all big prehistoric animals were dinosaurs, however.

Many other reptiles shared the Earth with the dinosaurs. Some swam in the seas and others flew through the air, but these were not dinosaurs. The dinosaurs could not swim or fly – they lived on land or perhaps in shallow marshes.

Dinosaurs' legs were different from those of most reptiles. They extended straight down below the dinosaur's body, holding it up off the ground. Many dinosaurs could probably run well. Other reptiles had legs that splayed out sideways (like lizards and crocodiles today). These reptiles dragged their bodies along the ground and probably could not move as well as dinosaurs.

How do we know about dinosaurs?

Their bones and teeth are preserved as fossils in the rocks. But that is all we know about for sure. No one has ever seen living dinosaurs. Was their skin brightly colored or dull and drab? How long did they live? Could they make any sounds? How did they behave? Exactly what did they eat? We can make good guesses about dinosaurs, using the sorts of methods described in this book. But we will probably never know for sure.

A well-known dinosaur

Iguanodon *is one of the dinosaurs we know most about. Thousands of its fossilized bones have been found across Europe and in Asia, in rocks about 120 million years old. In some fossil skeletons, every bone in the body is preserved. Remains of* Iguanodon-*like dinosaurs have also been found in North and South America, Africa, and Australia.*

Why no front teeth?
Iguanodon had no front teeth. The front parts of its jawbones were shaped like a hard "beak." This would be no good for eating meat and so was probably used to chop leaves and stems.

Telltale back teeth
Iguanodon's back teeth were broad and flat, similar to the teeth of plant-eating animals today. Adding this evidence to the clues from the "beak," we are fairly sure that *Iguanodon* ate plants and not meat. *(You can find out more about plant-eaters on page 44.)*

A handy pair of hands
For dinosaurs that walked mainly on their back legs, the arms were left free to do other jobs. *Iguanodon* had hooflike middle fingers, possibly to lean on as it bent down to eat. Its smallest finger was separate and could have been used to grasp food. Perhaps it used its spiky thumb to defend itself against meat-eating enemies.

Scaly skin

Usually the soft parts of an animal like the skin rot away quickly, before they can be preserved as fossils. In a few dinosaur finds the texture of the skin has been pressed into the rocks, showing that it was scaly and tough. But it's impossible to know what color the skin was, or whether it had spots or stripes.

Sharp eyes and ears?

Skull bones show the general shape of a dinosaur's head, but we have to guess at soft parts like eyes, ears, and nostrils. We don't know if *Iguanodon* had good sight or hearing. But its many fossils show that this creature probably lived in great numbers. *(You can find out more about skulls on pages 44-45.)*

How big was the brain?

We can estimate the size of a dinosaur's brain from the size of the "hole" inside the fossilized skull bones. Like reptiles of today, *Iguanodon* and many other dinosaurs had small brains compared to their big bodies. But we have no way of knowing for certain how intelligent they were.

Two legs or four?

Even though we have found so many fossils of *Iguanodon*, experts cannot agree about whether it walked on two legs or four. It probably walked on its two back legs, but it might have occasionally stooped down and grazed on all fours, like a kangaroo of today.

5

Iguanodon
Here and on other pages you can see how big dinosaurs would be compared with humans – if we'd been around at the time! *Iguanodon* was about 33 feet (10m) long and weighed 2 to 4 tons.

A bulky body?
Iguanodon would have had to eat huge amounts of plants to keep itself going, and its stomach and intestines would have needed to be enormous to digest all this food. So its body was probably very bulky. Some plant-eating dinosaurs may have swallowed stones to help grind up the food in their stomach.

Why are hipbones important?

Experts divide dinosaurs into two main groups, depending mainly on the shape of the hipbones. This division may not seem important, but it is vital to the scientific study of dinosaurs. One group is called the *Saurischia,* or "lizard-hipped" dinosaurs. In these the long thin hipbone called the pubis pointed downward and forward, in line with the back leg bones, as it does in lizards today. The other group is the *Ornithischia,* or "bird-hipped" dinosaurs. Here the pubis pointed downward and backward, as it does in today's birds (hence the name "bird-hipped"). As you can see from the picture, *Iguanodon* was a bird-hipped dinosaur.

A tail to lean on?

Dinosaur tails mostly look quite similar. Yet, like other parts of the body, the tail may have had special uses. *Iguanodon* probably lifted its tail off the ground as it ran, using it as a counterweight to help it balance. The tail could also have been a "seat" for *Iguanodon* to lean on as it ate leaves from trees.

7

DISCOVERING DINOSAURS

When an animal or plant dies, several things can happen. Its body may be eaten by other animals, or slowly rot away. Sometimes, though, its remains are washed into a river or lake, and are buried by mud. Or they may be buried under windblown sand in a desert. As time passes, more and more mud or sand piles up on top, pressing on the remains. Gradually the sand and mud turn into rock. Chemicals in the rocks seep into the remains, harden them, and turn them into rock, too. The remains have become *fossils*.

Fossils take thousands of years to form. Any animal or plant can become a fossil. Usually, however, the soft parts, like the skin, stomach, and muscles, rot away too quickly to be fossilized. Only hard parts, like shells, bones, and teeth, are preserved – though they are often crushed and broken in the process. The hard parts of plants, like seeds and tiny pollen grains, also become fossils.

Fossils can also form in other ways. Sometimes a soft part of the body, like skin, is covered so quickly (perhaps in a mudslide) that all of its details are preserved. Later the remains rot away and the "hole" left in the rock becomes filled with stone. An animal's dung or its footprints can also become fossils. It is mainly from fossils that we know about life in the past. Dinosaurs, being big, have left many fossils in the rocks. The problem is how to find them and dig them out without breaking them.

The excitement of the "dig"

Sometimes fossils are found lying on the surface of the ground. More often they are still buried, perhaps showing at the side of a cliff. The first clues may be bits of fossil bones falling to the bottom of a cliff, or dug up by farmers or quarry workers. Soon the site, called a "dig," is busy with teams of experts.

Rock removal
Large chunks of soil and rock can be moved by diggers and bulldozers. But as the fossils are slowly uncovered, the work is done more carefully, using shovels, drills, hammers, and chisels.

Making records
Before the bones are removed they are measured and notes, drawings, and photos are made of them. Accurate diagrams are needed to put the bones back together again later.

The end of the tail
Follow this tail back to the previous two pages to see the rest of *Iguanodon*.

Digging into the past
As sand, mud, and silt sink to the bottom of rivers, lakes, and seas, they pile up in layers. Their tremendous weight squashes the layers below

Bandages for broken bones

A weak or crumbly bone is sprayed with a hard-setting foam or strapped in plaster-soaked bandages. When hard, the bone is lifted and its base is treated in the same way. It is now safe to move.

Back to the laboratory

Fossils are often found in remote, hilly places. They are put carefully into padded crates and lifted into a truck, then taken by road, train, or plane back to the laboratory.

Free at last!

Some bones can be gently chiseled free of the surrounding rock. Or a block containing many small bones may be lifted away. Every piece is numbered and recorded.

into rock. Each layer is slightly different from the others, and the oldest layers are at the bottom. Fossils are trapped in each layer. Because animals and plants change over time, the fossils in each layer are also slightly different. *Paleontologists* (fossil experts) can work out the age of the various rocks and the fossils usually found in them.

We can also work out the age of rocks by measuring the tiny amounts of radioactivity they contain. Only rocks 65 to 205 million years old contain fossils of dinosaurs.

REBUILDING A DINOSAUR

Rebuilding a dinosaur is a slow process. It can take years to clean the rock from the fossil bones and teeth. Squashed and broken bones must be pieced together, missing parts determined, and all the bones assembled into a skeleton. Dinosaurs are rebuilt from the bones outward. The next task is to decide what the soft parts of the body, such as the brain, muscles, stomach and digestive organs, fat and skin, looked like. The fossil bones are compared with other fossils and with the bones of living reptiles and other animals, to find out where the dinosaur's muscles were attached to its skeleton and how its joints worked.

Getting the bones out of the rock is especially difficult. Every trace of rock must be removed – yet the bone must not be marked or damaged in any way, or mistakes could be made when working out the muscles and soft parts. Many tools are used, from hammers and chisels to ultrasonic tools that shatter the rock with high-power sound waves, high-speed whistling drills (like those your dentist uses), miniature sand-blasters, pneumatic chisels like tiny road drills, and fast-shaking "vibropens." Sometimes acids can be used to dissolve the rock, provided they won't harm the fossil itself.

A giant jigsaw puzzle

Imagine rebuilding a dinosaur. It would be like doing a giant jigsaw puzzle, with some pieces missing and others broken. Here a team of miniature workers are fitting bones together to rebuild a Stegosaurus *skeleton.*

Rods and wires

Fossil bones are solid rock, so they are very heavy. Plastic or metal rods can be bent to the shape of a leg or backbone, to hold it in position. Scaffolds and wires from the ceiling support the highest parts.

Bone or hole?

Dinosaur skulls are made of many separate bones, which sometimes have spaces between them. But is there really a space, or is a bone missing? Bones with teeth must be the jaws, so they are a good starting point to work from.

Missing bones

Complete fossil skeletons, with all the bones, are very rare. If a missing bone is one of a pair, as in a leg, it can be modeled from its partner. If not, experts may "borrow" the bone shape from a dinosaur that looks similar.

Running repairs

Wide cracks are filled with plastic or plaster. Fragile bones can be strengthened with hard-setting plastic. Since fossils are heavy, light plastic or plaster models of them may be used. The real bones stay safe in storage.

Wrong bones

If the bones were jumbled up in the rock, finding the right place for each one is very tricky. At first, the thumb-claw of *Iguanodon* was thought to be a horn on its nose! Some bones may even be from a completely different animal.

Joined at the hip

Hipbones are important. They tell us which main group of dinosaurs the animal belonged to, whether it walked on two legs or four, and whether it held its body upright, tilted, or parallel to the ground.

Upside down?

Every dinosaur has the same basic bones, but their sizes and shapes differ. Which way up does a leg bone go, and is it part of the front or back leg? Shallow marks on the bones show where muscles and ligaments were attached.

11

THE CHANGING WORLD

Ever since the Earth formed, about 4,500 million years ago, it has been constantly but very slowly changing. Daily changes in the weather bring wind, rain, and ice, which gradually wear down mountains and fill in valleys. Not only that, the land under our feet is actually moving, although far too slowly for us to notice. The surface of the Earth is made of many layers called "plates," hundreds of miles across, like pieces in a giant curved jigsaw puzzle. Very slowly, at most a few inches a year, the plates move. At the bottom of the oceans molten rock wells up from inside the Earth. As it rises between two plates, it pushes them apart and joins onto the edges of the plates. At the same time, in other places on Earth the plates are being destroyed or squeezed together. As plates crack, volcanoes erupt. As they rub past each other, there are earthquakes. Into this ever-changing world, about 205 million years ago, came the dinosaurs.

The Earth through the ages
Throughout time, the continents have been changing position, coming together then moving apart again very slowly. Plant and animal life have changed at the same time.

Triassic Period
225 to 193 million years ago, the first dinosaurs appeared. Reptiles had already been around for 100 million years.

Jurassic Period
193 to 136 million years ago, there were dinosaurs of all shapes and sizes. Lush vegetation covered much of the land.

Cretaceous Period
136 to 65 million years ago was the heyday of the dinosaurs. Hundreds of different kinds lived all over the world.

North America

South America

Cenozoic Era
After the death of the dinosaurs, mammals took over. The Age of Mammals began 65 million years ago.

Today
One mammal now dominates the world. This is the Age of Man.

Carboniferous Period
Amphibians roamed swampy forests of giant ferns 300 million years ago.

Pangaea

Laurasia

Gondwanaland

Europe and Asia

Africa

India

North America

Europe

Asia

India

Africa

South America

325 million years ago
There were only three huge land masses, instead of the seven continents there are today.

200 million years ago
All the land masses had moved together to form one "super-continent," Pangaea. Evidence for this comes from fossils of the same land animals found on different continents today. In those days these animals could simply walk from place to place.

135 million years ago
When dinosaurs ruled the world, two continents were forming, as Pangaea had split into two. Laurasia was moving northward. Gondwanaland, drifting south, was made of what are now South America, Africa, Arabia, India, Antarctica, and Australia.

80 million years ago
Gradually the super-continents broke up. Africa and South America were separated by the opening of the Atlantic Ocean but North America was still joined to Europe and Asia. India was moving away from Africa toward Asia.

7 million years ago
The continents were now in their present positions. Antarctica was centered on the South Pole, and North and South America were still joined by a narrow strip of land. This formed a land bridge for animals and they migrated both north and south.

The world today
Great forces still move the continents, changing the face of the Earth.

13

LIFE BEFORE THE DINOSAURS

There were many forms of life on Earth before the dinosaurs. In the warm, shallow seas, chemicals came together to make the first living things. Gradually, over a long period of time, some of these joined together to make bigger and more complicated living things. The first plants were followed by the first animals, which were plant-eaters. Then came the animals that ate other animals. Life continued to change, or *evolve*, and many weird and wonderful creatures appeared – jellyfish, worms, snails, and fish. How do we know? Like the dinosaurs, many of these early animals

1 The Earth forms
About 6,000 million years ago dust, gases, and bits of rock and minerals whirled through space. Gradually they were brought together by the force of gravity to form a solid ball, the Earth, which orbited continuously around the Sun.

2 The first life
As the Earth cooled, life appeared in the warm seas. The first living things we know of were probably similar to the blue-green algae and bacteria of today. Their microscopic remains have been found in African rocks 3,200 million years old.

Early plants

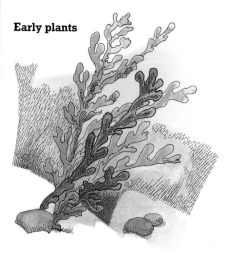

3 Bigger and better
Living things gradually became bigger and more complicated. Fossils of them are rare because they had soft bodies. However, remains from Australia show that 670 million years ago jellyfish and worms lived in the sea.

Jellyfish

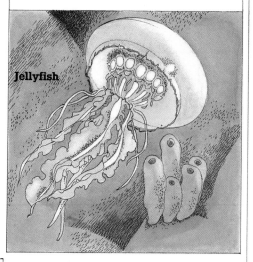

7 The first land plants
The first plants lived in water. Over millions of years they evolved a waterproof covering and stiff stems, so they were able to grow on land. *Cooksonia,* an early land plant, had no leaves, flowers, or roots and was only a few inches tall.

Cooksonia

8 The amphibians arrive
Amphibians live both on land and in the water. The first ones evolved from fish and appeared about 370 million years ago. At first they still had a fishy shape, then they came to look like lizards. They had to return to water to lay their eggs.

Ichthyostega

9 Mammal-like reptiles
Reptiles became more numerous than the amphibians about 280 million years ago. One of the first groups to flourish was the "mammal-like reptiles." Experts think that these gradually evolved into animals related to mammals.

Dimetrodon

became fossilized. Even those with soft bodies were occasionally preserved. Perhaps an underwater avalanche of mud covered them and hardened before their bodies had time to rot away. Such "lucky accidents" give us a fascinating glimpse into life on Earth before the dinosaurs.

The game of life
Animals are always evolving to fit their surroundings better, but the surroundings are constantly changing too. This is why animal life has changed over the years.

4 The first shellfish
About 570 million years ago the first shelled animals appeared. Among them were brachiopods (lamp-shells), which were common for millions of years. These had two shells to protect the soft, delicate parts inside.

Brachiopods

5 The beginning of the backbone
The evolution of a backbone was a great advance, as it meant creatures could move around more. The first *vertebrates* (animals with backbones) were fish, some 500 million years ago. They had good eyesight and bony armor.

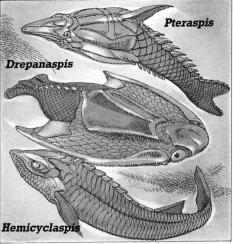
Pteraspis
Drepanaspis
Hemicyclaspis

6 Fish out of water
One goup of fish had fleshy, lobed fins. They were able to use their fins like limbs to move over mud, and could breathe air, as they had lungs. About 370 million years ago, they first crawled out on to land.

Eusthenopteron

10 The first hums and buzzes
Like plants, insects appeared on land well before the amphibians. In fact they were food for the first amphibians. By 300 million years ago there were cockroaches and giant dragonflies with wings up to 2 feet (60cm) across.

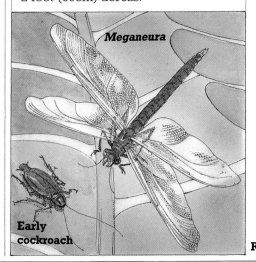
Meganeura
Early cockroach

11 The reptiles branch out
By about 200 million years ago there were many different kinds of reptiles. One of the most common groups was the rhynchosaurs. These were about the same size as sheep and chewed plants with their chisel-like teeth.

Rhynchosaurs

12 Ancestors of the dinosaurs
Another early group of reptiles was the thecodonts, which evolved over 220 million years ago. At first they were crocodilelike creatures, but they gradually began to walk on two legs. These were probably the ancestors of the dinosaurs.

Thecodont

THE FIRST DINOSAURS

About 220 million years ago, several groups of big reptiles roamed the world. One group was the thecodonts. They had straighter legs than other reptiles and sharp flesh-tearing teeth, and spent a lot of their time in water. Many were similar to the crocodiles of today, and in fact their ancestors were also the ancestors of our crocodiles. They also gave rise to another group of reptiles – the dinosaurs.

By 205 million years ago, dinosaurs were evolving from thecodont-like reptiles. They held their limbs straight under their bodies, and some could move quickly on their back legs and use their tails for balancing. Soon the two great groups of dinosaurs appeared – the lizard-hipped saurischians and the bird-hipped ornithischians (*see page 7*).

First came the saurischians, which we divide into two groups. One group, including the prosauropods such as *Plateosaurus*, was probably related to the giant four-legged plant-eating sauropods (*see pages 24-25*). The other group was the theropods, like *Coelophysis*, which walked on two legs and hunted for meat.

Dinosaurs walking tall

One way in which dinosaurs differed from other reptiles was that their legs were held straight under their bodies instead of sprawling out sideways.

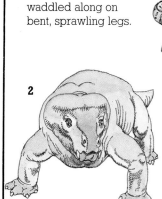

1 Lizard
Then, as now, lizards waddled along on bent, sprawling legs.

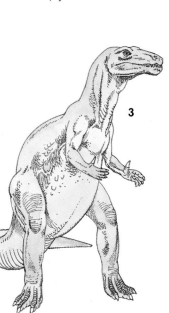

2 Thecodont
These dinosaur forerunners had legs more under the body.

3 Dinosaur
The legs were tucked well under the body, supporting its weight.

Two early dinosaurs
The large, lumbering Plateosaurus, *from Europe, and the smaller, sleeker* Coelophysis, *from the southwestern U.S., were among the first dinosaurs. Both of them lived just over 200 million years ago.*

Always a plant-eater?
Judging by their fossil remains, prosauropods were the first of the large plant-eating dinosaurs and lived in most parts of the world. The early prosauropods may have been small two-legged hunters. Members like *Plateosaurus* probably ate plants and could have walked on two or four legs.

Plateosaurus

Leaves for lunch
Plateosaurus probably ate leaves, shredding them with its rows of small teeth. Maybe it used its sharply clawed front legs to gather food, or to defend itself. *Plateosaurus* was over 26 feet (8m) long, and when standing on its back legs it could reach as high as 15 to 20 feet (5-6m).

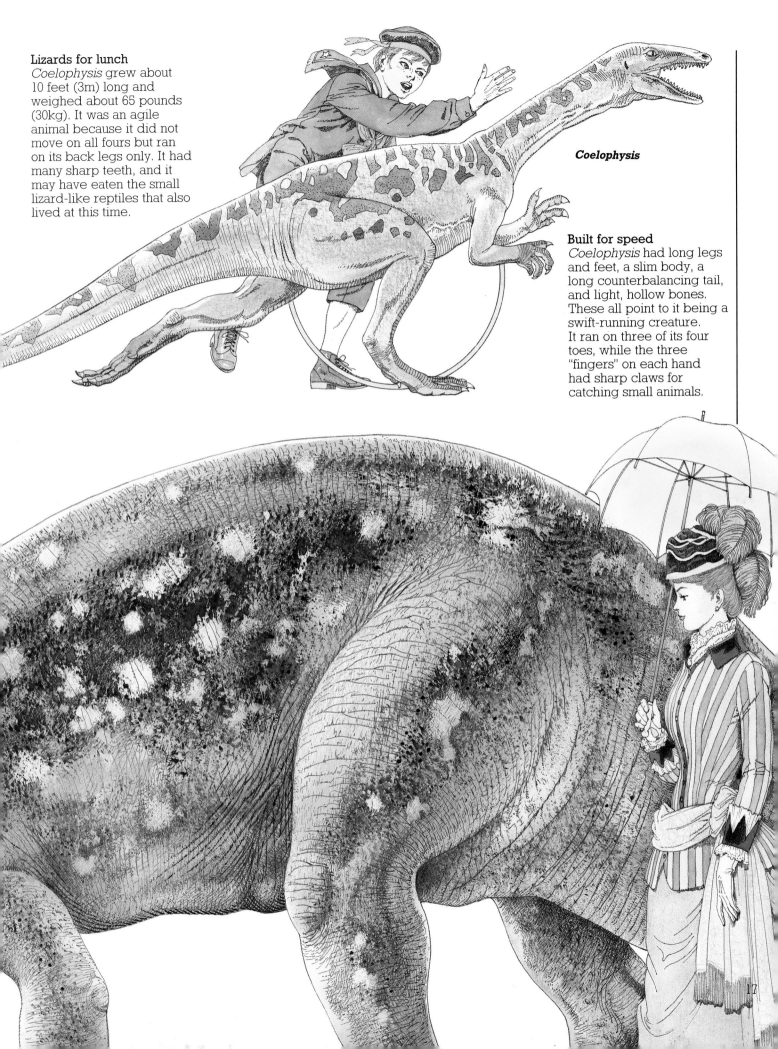

Lizards for lunch
Coelophysis grew about 10 feet (3m) long and weighed about 65 pounds (30kg). It was an agile animal because it did not move on all fours but ran on its back legs only. It had many sharp teeth, and it may have eaten the small lizard-like reptiles that also lived at this time.

Coelophysis

Built for speed
Coelophysis had long legs and feet, a slim body, a long counterbalancing tail, and light, hollow bones. These all point to it being a swift-running creature. It ran on three of its four toes, while the three "fingers" on each hand had sharp claws for catching small animals.

THE AGE OF DINOSAURS

At the beginning of the Age of Dinosaurs, the world was mostly hot and dry. Gradually the climate altered as the continents moved (*see page 12*). New animals and plants evolved. Some flourished, others died out. As the weather became warmer and wetter, plant fossils tell us, there were great forests of giant ferns, stumpy palmlike cycads, and various conifers such as yews, cypresses, and monkey-puzzle trees. In this ever-changing world, the dinosaurs changed too. Then, around 100 million years ago, flowers and blossom trees appeared. Soon there were forests of magnolia, laurel, and oak. Birds, insects, and other creatures evolved to feed on the nectar and pollen in the new flowers. By the end of the Age of Dinosaurs, the world was a very different place.

The late Jurassic scene
It is late in the Jurassic Period, about 140 million years ago. The dinosaurs have already been on Earth for more than 60 million years, and have evolved into creatures with diverse ways of life. In their world live many other reptiles, as well as mammals and the first birds.

Ceratosaurus

Stegosaurus

Mammals

Lizard

Meat to eat
The large plant-eating dinosaurs were meals on legs for the flesh-eating dinosaurs like *Allosaurus.* Meat-eaters needed to be quick and well-armed with teeth and claws.

Survival of the fittest
Just as today, life was a struggle and only the fittest survived. The huge *Stegosaurus*, with its egg-sized brain, was probably not too clever. Yet it lived for millions of years.

Mammals
The first mammals appeared not long after the first dinosaurs. Furry and warm-blooded, they looked for food at night, when most reptiles were too cold to move quickly.

Sauropods
The giant plant-eating dinosaurs, the sauropods, were very common (*see page 24*). *Apatosaurus* browsed in herds, snipping leaves off trees with its peglike teeth.

Lizards and turtles
Neither of these groups of reptiles has changed much over the millions of years since the Age of Dinosaurs. Lizards probably fed on small creatures and insects.

Pterosaurs
These "winged lizards" were not dinosaurs or lizards, but reptiles. They were masters of the air for 140 million years, and some may have had fur and possibly warm blood.

Turtle

Ready for take-off
Any number of dinosaurs were ready to pounce on *Archaeopteryx* (*see page 56*). *The need to escape predators may have led to the evolution of bird flight.*

Small-time thief
Ornitholestes, or "bird robber," was typical of the small, agile dinosaurs that ate any kind of tidbit – insects, frogs, lizards, a reptile or bird's egg, or even a baby dinosaur!

Ornitholestes

9

Life in the late Cretaceous Period

The Age of Dinosaurs began to draw to a close during the late Cretaceous Period, about 70 million years ago. The dinosaurs themselves were still numerous and varied. From three "family groups" 200 million years ago, sixteen had now developed. The animals and plants that lived alongside the dinosaurs were also changing. Pterosaurs shared the skies with various birds. Some cycad, fern, and conifer forests had been replaced by trees bearing flowers and fruits, while herbs and wild flowers carpeted the ground.

The "terror croc"

Crocodiles were around before the dinosaurs. *Deinosuchus*, from Texas, had a skull nearly 6½ feet (2m) long. The whole animal may have been some 40 feet (12m) long.

The early birds

Some of the first bird groups to evolve were probably the gulls, ducks, and waders. *Ichthyornis* was the same size as the common gull of today, and had similar seaside habits.

Ichthyornis

Deinosuchus

Turtles

Butterflies

The birds go fishing

Hesperornis was a fish-eating bird about 3 feet (1m) tall. It had teeth along its beak, to hold its slippery prey firm, and was a strong swimmer.

Biding their time

Many mammals had appeared by now, including shrewlike insect-eaters. Small and timid, they were still completely overshadowed by the dinosaurs.

Hadrosaurs
The "duck-billed" dinosaurs were one of the last groups to evolve (*see page 44*). Their general shape shows they were at home wading through lagoons and swamps.

Ceratopians
Fossils of the horned dinosaurs, such as *Triceratops*, show they had all types of horns and frilly neckplates. Presumably these were protection against enemies.

Buzzing and flitting
Bees, butterflies, and moths probably appeared at about the same time as the first flowering plants. In return for nectar, the insects took pollen from flower to flower.

King of the carnivores
Tyrannosaurus, at 46 feet (14m), was the biggest flesh-eating animal ever to walk the Earth (*see page 48*). It may have fed on carrion (animals already dead).

Triceratops

Bees

FOOTPRINTS IN TIME

Bones are not the only things to become fossils. The signs of where animals have been are also often fossilized – their footprints and the furrows where their tails drag. Many tracks have been found which were probably made by dinosaurs walking in soft sand or mud, perhaps going down to a river to drink. After they had passed, the sun dried the mud and baked it hard. Later on, maybe during a flood, more mud settled on top. The prints were gradually buried and turned to stone. Fossil dinosaur tracks have been discovered in many places, including southeastern England, western Canada, New England and Texas, Australia and Brazil. At first, people thought the tracks had been made by giants or gods. But when scientists began to realize that dinosaurs had existed, the prints could be explained. In fact they give us a lot of information. An expert may be able to tell whether the creature moved on two legs or four, how fast it was going, and if it was walking or running.

Travelling in herds
Many sets of similar footprints made at the same time suggest that dinosaurs sometimes traveled in herds. In Texas 23 sets of prints, 120 million years old, were probably made by large plant-eaters like *Apatosaurus*.

Walk this way . . .
Dinosaur prints like these are found in rocks that were once sand or mud. In a 3¾-mile (6-km) length of Peace River Canyon in Canada, there are over 1,700 footprints, made by ten different kinds of dinosaurs. It was a busy place!

Where's the tail?
Each footprint is huge – about 3 feet (1m) long – but although *Apatosaurus* had a long tail, there are no signs of tail furrows. Perhaps they waded through water with their tails floating or held their tails off the ground.

The pack in pursuit
Beneath and on top of the *Apatosaurus* tracks, there are footprints of a herd of three-toed carnivorous dinosaurs. They must have been around while the ground was muddy and may have been hunting the *Apatosaurus*.

Stride and speed

Experts work out how fast dinosaurs moved from the space between footprints (the stride) and their depth. Medium-sized meat-eaters could run at about 10 miles (16km) per hour, and plant-eaters ran at about 3¾ miles (6km) per hour.

Family outing

At Peace River there are many sets of prints, made by hadrosaur-type dinosaurs. The bigger footprints were made first and the smaller ones afterward. Was it a family outing, with the youngsters following their parents? The same site also shows prints of meat-eaters.

Meat-eaters

The lone hunter

Tyrannosaurus-type footprints have been discovered in several places. Unlike the prints of smaller meat-eaters, there are only one or two sets at a time, so *Tyrannosaurus* probably hunted either on its own or in pairs.

THE BIGGEST OF ALL

The sauropod dinosaurs were the biggest animals ever to roam the land. Various kinds of sauropods lived almost throughout the Age of Dinosaurs, from over 200 million years ago until the great extinction about 65 million years ago. Yet these gigantic creatures were all slow, small-brained plant-eaters. They had barrel-shaped bodies, long necks and tails, and walked on all fours. *Brachiosaurus* is probably the biggest discovered so far. Its weight is guessed at 77 tons. Even so, it is probably not the largest animal ever. The record-holder is the blue whale, which is swimming in the oceans today. Blue whales may grow to over 100 feet (30m) long and weigh nearly 200 tons.

The dinosaurs are in town!
To give you an idea of their size, three of the biggest sauropods are shown arriving in town. People used to think they lived in rivers or swamps, but experts now believe they walked on land.

The longest dinosaur
Diplodocus is one of the longest dinosaurs found so far. Its neck was 26 feet (8m) long, its body 16½ feet (5m), and its tail 46 feet (14m). Yet it was a slim animal, weighing only 10 tons. Its weak teeth could strip leaves from trees but not chew them. Like other sauropods, *Diplodocus* may have had a gizzard – a strong "stomach" to grind its food to shreds.

The "thunder lizard"
Apatosaurus has had a confusing history. Its fossil bones were mixed up with those of another sauropod called *Camarasaurus*, and it used to be commonly known as *Brontosaurus* ("thunder lizard"). It was almost 70 feet (21m) long and weighed about 30 tons.

Biggest – so far

Brachiosaurus was the heaviest dinosaur and may have been even longer than *Diplodocus*. Bones that have been found of two other dinosaurs, nicknamed *"Supersaurus"* and *"Ultrasaurus,"* suggest they may have been even bigger than *Brachiosaurus*.

Advantages of being big

With its long neck, a sauropod could pluck food from high in trees, where others could not reach. And predators would think twice before attacking such a huge animal.

Apatosaurus

25

THE SMALLEST DINOSAURS

One of the remarkable things about dinosaurs is that they came in so many shapes – and sizes. From giants taller than a house, they ranged down to mini-dinosaurs no bigger than modern-day chickens. Why were some so small? Probably for the same reasons that some animals today are small. It is easier for a small animal to hide from predators, in the undergrowth or in a crack in the rocks. And, for a reptile, a smaller body warms up more quickly in the morning sun, so that the animal is ready for action sooner.

There may be fossil bones and teeth of even tinier dinosaurs waiting to be discovered, but it is very hard to find them. When a small animal dies, if it is eaten, it is more likely to be eaten whole, including its bones. If it is not eaten, the small and fragile bones are quite likely to be crushed and broken as they are sealed in rock and fossilized. And, in searches for new fossil sites, small bones are more likely to be overlooked than larger ones – even by the experts!

Saltopus

Compsognathus

Small but speedy
The dinosaurs shown here lived in different places on the Earth, at different times, and belonged to different groups. But they all have one thing in common: they are among the smallest dinosaurs discovered so far.

26

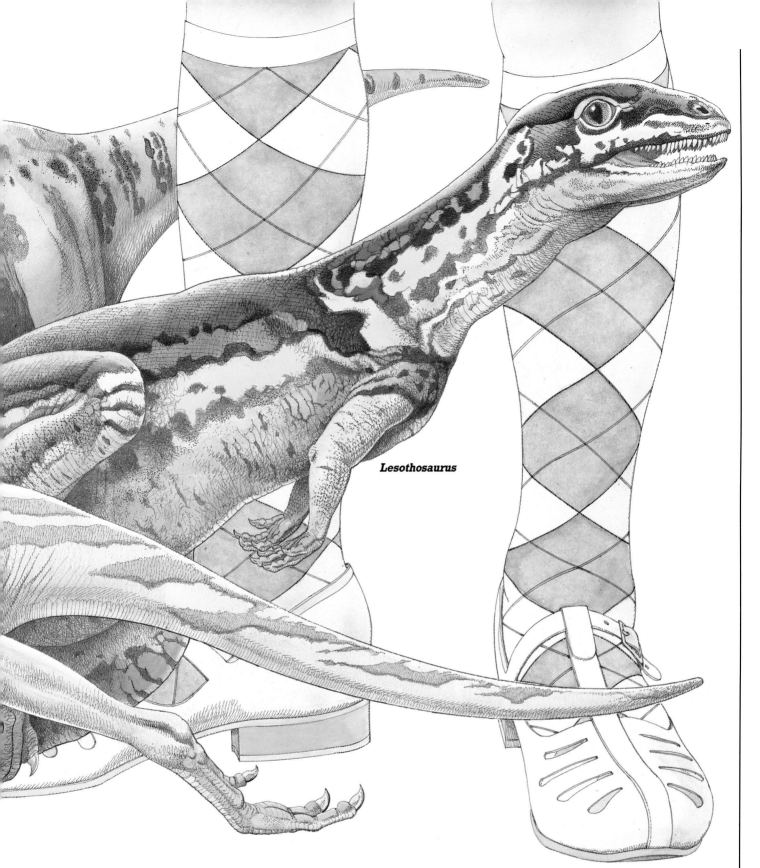

Lesothosaurus

Saltopus ("leaping foot")

This animal was 2 feet (60cm) long
and weighed 2 pounds (1kg). Slim
and agile, it probably ate small
creatures such as insects. It lived
around 200 million years ago and was
one of the very early dinosaurs,
related to *Coelophysis*. Its fossils
have been found only in Scotland.

Compsognathus ("pretty jaw")

Over 2 feet (60cm) long and weighing
6½ pounds (3kg), this dinosaur lived
145 million years ago. Its remains
have been found in Germany and
France. In one case, small lizard bones
were found where *Compsognathus*'s
stomach would have been, which
suggests its last meal.

Lesothosaurus ("Lesotho lizard")

This little dinosaur, only 3 feet (90cm)
long, had long, slim legs and a thin
tail. Its fossils were found in Lesotho,
in southern Africa, where it lived
nearly 200 million years ago. Flat,
leaf-shaped teeth and a "beak" at the
front of its mouth suggest that it
probably fed on plants.

THE WEALDEN SCENE

In prehistoric times, the land that now forms south-eastern England, northern France, and northern Belgium was a low, flat plain – a "weald." Marsh plants grew thickly in the swampy ground and animals lived among them, eating the plants and each other. Rivers from the north carried mud and sand out on to the plain. Over thousands of years the water level rose and fell, and the swamps came and went. The sand and mud were slowly buried and pressed down into sandstone and clay. In them, preserved as fossils, were the remains of the plants and animals that had lived on the Weald. Then, 120 million years later, a tooth of one of these creatures saw the light of day again. It was dug from a gravel pit near Lewes, in Sussex, and noticed by a local doctor named Gideon Mantell. Puzzling over it, he noticed it was similar to the tooth of a modern-day iguana lizard – though much larger. He named the unknown creature it came from *Iguanodon*. And so, in about 1822, the first dinosaur fossil was found.

Dinosaurs in southeast England
The clays and rocks of the Wealden area have been a treasure trove for fossil-hunters. Dr. Mantell, a keen geologist, began the discoveries that allow us to re-create this scene from the past.

The discovery of "Claws"
In 1982 another amateur fossil-hunter, William Walker, discovered a huge stone claw in a Surrey quarry. Soon, parts of a dinosaur skeleton were also found. Nicknamed "Claws," the dinosaur was officially called *Baryonyx walkeri*, "heavy claw of Walker," in honor of its discoverer.

Baryonyx was a large theropod, or flesh-eater, that lived 124 million years ago. It is the most complete large theropod of that age to be found anywhere in the world. Its famous claw measures about 12 inches (31cm) along the outside edge, but it's not clear whether it was on the dinosaur's hand or foot.

Running away from danger
The plant-eating *Hypsilophodon*, only 6½ feet (2m) tall, had little defense against big predators. Its build suggests that it simply ran away from danger, using its long, stiff tail to help keep its balance.

A Wealden favorite

Herds of *Iguanodon* roamed the Wealden landscape, chomping on the soft vegetation. Many fossil skeletons have been found here, as well as footprints. *(You can find out more about Iguanodon on pages 4-7.)*

Food for all

The main plants eaten by the Wealden dinosaurs were low-growing mosses and liverworts, conifer trees, cycads (which look like palm trees with fern leaves), and giant tree ferns that grew to 60 feet (18m) in height.

On the way out?

Around this time the large meat-eater *Megalosaurus* seemed to be dying out. This was the first dinosaur to be scientifically described, by William Buckland in 1824. It was a two-legged meat-eater.

Crocodiles

Thick skin and spines

Polacanthus, an ankylosaur (*see page 38*), was 13 feet (4m) long and had armor-plated skin and sharp protective spines. Its skull has never been discovered, and the positions of the spines are largely guesswork.

FLYING REPTILES

Dinosaurs never flew. But their reptile cousins, the pterosaurs, dominated the skies for almost as long as the dinosaurs ruled the land. The pterosaurs were not the first flying creatures, however. For millions of years insects such as giant dragonflies had droned through the air. But the pterosaurs were much larger than insects. In fact one pterosaur, *Quetzalcoatlus*, was the biggest flying animal ever. From wingtip to wingtip it may have measured almost 50 feet (15m).

When the pterosaurs evolved, there were two main groups. One group, the rhamphorhynchoids, appeared about 200 million years ago. The rhamphorhynchoids were long reptiles with teeth and a tail. The second group, the pterodactyloids, evolved 150 million years ago and lasted until the extinction of the dinosaurs 65 million years ago. These reptiles had no tail, but some had teeth and some had crests on their heads.

Gliders or flappers?
When fossil pterosaur bones were first found, people thought pterosaurs lived in the sea, like penguins! Then experts believed they could only glide, jumping from clifftops and using rising currents of air to gain height, like hang gliders. Now we think some could have been active fliers.

How big was the brain?
Fossilized skull bones show that pterosaurs had large eyes and big brains. The part of the brain dealing with muscle coordination was especially large, probably to control the various muscles needed for flight.

What did they eat?
Some pterosaurs had teeth arranged for scooping and sieving small creatures from sea water. *Pteranodon* ("winged and toothless") had no teeth, so perhaps it plucked fish from the surface of the sea, like some seabirds today.

A hairy body?
Active flight demands lots of energy, which suggests some pterosaurs were warm-blooded. Traces of hair have been found on some remains, which supports the idea of warm-bloodedness (*see pages 54-55*).

A rudder for steering?
Rhamphorhynchoids had a long tail with a kite-shaped end. This probably acted as a rudder for steering. Perhaps the head crest of *Pteranodon* did the same job – or it could have been to tell which were males and which females.

Pteranodon

This large crested pterosaur had a wingspan of 23 feet (7m), but its body was only about the size of a turkey. It weighed less than 44 pounds (20kg). A pterodactyloid, it lived around 70 million years ago.

Rhamphorhynchus

Many fine fossils of this pterosaur have been found in Germany, in rocks 140 million years old. Its name means "narrow beak." It had a tail and forward-pointing teeth in its beak-shaped jaws.

Quetzalcoatlus

This enormous pterodactyl had the long face, long neck, and short tail typical of its group. Although named "feathered serpent," after an Aztec god, it had no feathers. Its fossils were first found in 1972, in Texas.

Could they flap?

Pterosaurs had a strong breastbone to anchor powerful wing muscles. Most of the wing was held out on the bones of a very long fourth finger. Fossil evidence suggests that some pterosaurs could flap their wings.

SEA REPTILES

Some dinosaurs waded through swamps, and a few probably swam in lakes and rivers. No dinosaurs, as far as we know, lived in the sea. Yet when dinosaurs ruled the land, their cousins, the big and fierce swimming reptiles, ruled the waves. There were three main groups. The ichthyosaurs were completely at home in the water, with a streamlined shape, finlike arms, and legs like a fish's tail. The ichthyosaurs were very numerous and lived from 220 to 90 million years ago. A second group of reptiles, the plesiosaurs, had four paddlelike limbs and a pointed tail. They also appeared about 220 million years ago, dying out with the dinosaurs. The fearsome mosasaur, with its sharp teeth and a tail like a crocodile, was in the third group. It lived toward the end of the Age of Dinosaurs.

Lords of the open ocean
The great sea reptiles breathed air, like dinosaurs, so they would have had to swim to the surface of the water regularly to breathe. Fossilized ichthyosaurs from Germany reveal fish and pterosaur remains inside them.

Sticking its neck out
Elasmosaurus was a long-necked type of plesiosaur. The neck made up half of its total length of 43 feet (13m). It had a small head and sharp teeth, and it probably fed by darting its neck to and fro, snatching fish from near the surface of the sea.

Down in the depths
The short-necked plesiosaur *Liopleurodon* probably lived in deeper water than its long-necked relatives, feeding on turtles and shellfish. The largest reached almost 40 feet (12m) and had daggerlike teeth 4 inches (10cm) long.

The "fish lizard"
The body shape, flippers, and tail of *Ichthyosaurus* made it admirably suited to life in the water – just like today's dolphin. Up to 30 feet (9m) long, its fossils suggest it hunted in packs, eating squidlike creatures and fish.

An early turtle
Today's turtles are much like the first ones, known from fossils 220 million years old from Germany and Thailand. *Archelon* was one of the biggest, at nearly 13 feet (4m) long. It probably ate plants with its beaklike mouth.

The longest lizard
Mosasaurus, a type of lizard, grew to almost 30 feet (9m) – the longest "lizard" ever. It could open its huge mouth wide to devour anything it could catch. Fossils of ancient ammonites have been found with holes punched in them, probably by mosasaur teeth.

Ammonite

HORNS AND FRILLS

The horned dinosaurs, the Ceratopians, were one of the last main groups of dinosaurs. An early member was *Protoceratops*, or "first horned face." Its fossils have been found in the bleak Gobi Desert of Mongolia, in rocks more than 80 million years old. The most famous horned dinosaur was *Triceratops* (*shown on page 36*), which was still around at the end of the Age of Dinosaurs.

Ceratopians were bird-hipped dinosaurs and they were all plant-eaters. They must have tackled really tough food, since their jaws and skull bones were enormously strong. Their mouths were shaped like hooked beaks, probably for snipping off stringy leaves and shoots. Their numerous teeth were thin and sharp, forming a long blade in each jaw. The blades worked like shears to cut up food.

The strong muscles that worked the powerful jaws needed a wide, firm anchor. This may be why the neck frill developed. The frill also anchored the neck muscles and helped to protect the dinosaur. The skulls and frills were so strong that many fossils of them have been found in good condition.

On the defensive
These four horned dinosaurs from different times show how the body, frill and horns gradually became bigger. From an attacker's point of view they certainly looked fearsome and well protected!

Bumps before horns
One of the first horned dinosaurs, *Protoceratops* shows a stage in the group's evolution. It did not have true horns, only bony lumps on its skull. Also, its frill was smaller than in the later horned dinosaurs. It was about 6½ feet (2m) long. Fossils of its eggs and babies have been found.

Windows in the frill
Centrosaurus, or "sharp-point lizard," had many short spikes around the edge of its neck frill. Two larger spikes curved forward over "windows," which were holes in the frill bone covered by skin. These windows helped to make the dinosaur's head lighter than it would have been with a solid piece of bone. Like *Styracosaurus*, *Centrosaurus* was one of the group of short-frilled horned dinosaurs, which mostly lived earlier than the long-frilled types. *Centrosaurus* was about 20 feet (6m) long and lived 75 to 80 million years ago. Hundreds of its fossils were found in Canada.

Centrosaurus

Protoceratops

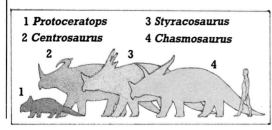

| 1 *Protoceratops* | 3 *Styracosaurus* |
| 2 *Centrosaurus* | 4 *Chasmosaurus* |

34

A spiky customer

Syracosaurus means "spiked lizard." Six long spikes pointed from its neck frill, as well as shorter spikes around the sides and a nose horn. It's likely that the nose horn was used as a weapon against attackers. The reason for the neck spikes is less clear. They could have been used to frighten enemies, or even to impress potential mates during the mating season. About 18 feet (5½m) long, *Styracosaurus* lived some 80 million years ago. Like other horned dinosaurs it had a fairly small tail, as it walked on all fours and therefore didn't need a big tail for balancing.

The "cleft lizard"

Chasmosaurus was a long-frilled horned dinosaur, about 16½ feet (5m) long. Its frill stretched halfway along its back and had enormous "windows" under the skin, making it look as though it was split in half. *Chasmosaurus* appeared about 80 million years ago and was one of the last dinosaurs to die out. All *Chasmosaurus* fossils have a nose horn, but some have short eyebrow horns while others have long ones (*as shown here*). Some experts believe there were two different kinds, or species. Others say the long-horned ones were males and the short-horned ones females.

Styracosaurus

Chasmosaurus

35

ON THE DEFENSE

Probably the most famous of the horned dinosaurs is *Triceratops.* It had three sharp horns – in fact its name means "three-horn face." What did *Triceratops* and its relatives (*shown on the previous pages*) use their horns for? As usual, when studying dinosaurs it helps to look at similar creatures alive today. The rhinoceros has a sharp horn on its nose, which it may use to defend itself against a predator. But the rhino's horn is mainly for show. It succeeds in frightening off enemies simply by its appearance, perhaps helped by charging in a threatening way toward the attacker. Scaring away predators makes more sense than getting into a real fight, where it risks being injured or killed. If worse came to worst, however, *Triceratops* might have used its horns to try to stab the enemy, being protected by its head shield and neck plate.

Safety in numbers

Fossilized footprints suggest that some horned dinosaurs like Triceratops *lived in herds. Perhaps they gathered into a tight group when a predator such as* Tyrannosaurus *came near, with the youngsters well protected behind the big, strong adults.*

Not an easy meal
Even one *Triceratops* on its own would not be an easy catch for a predator. Many fossils of *Triceratops* have been found in North America, in rocks about 70 million years old. They show that it was about 30 feet (9m) long and weighed over 5 tons – big enough to put up a good fight.

Surrounded!
A herd of adult *Triceratops* might have spread out to surround an enemy. A meat-eater such as *Tyrannosaurus* would not have been able to defend itself against all those sharp horns and it may have realized that retreat was the best answer.

A sign of strength
Besides using them for defense, *Triceratops* may have used its horns to battle with members of its own kind. Many horned creatures do this today, such as antelopes, rams, and deer. They charge at each other with a crash, or lock horns and wrestle in a trial of strength.

The "fights" rarely result in serious injury, though. They are to establish who is leader of the herd, or who has the right to mate with the females. Fossil *Triceratops* head frills have been found with damage that could have been caused by fights with another *Triceratops*.

DINOSAURS IN ARMOR

Some of the best-protected dinosaurs were the ankylosaurs. They were named after the biggest member of the group, *Ankylosaurus*, which grew up to 33 feet (10m) long and weighed as much as 5 tons. The name means "fused lizard," from the bony plates, lumps, and spines that covered these dinosaurs and protected them from meat-eaters. The plates were not part of the true skeleton. They developed from patches of thick skin that had fused and welded together. Some ankylosaurs had two "skulls" – the real one, and an outer one like the helmet in a suit of armor.

Two types of tails

Ankylosaurs are divided into two groups. Nodosaurids like Nodosaurus *had plenty of armor but no clublike tail weapon. Ankylosaurids, such as* Euoplocephalus, *had a bony club on the end of the tail.*

Ankylosaurs were bird-hipped dinosaurs (*see page 7*). Slow and lumbering, with small jaws and weak teeth, they probably ate soft plants. Inside the skull, bony flaps carried air from the nose to the back of the mouth, so that an ankylosaur could breathe and chew at the same time. The strong backbone and legs carried the weight of the armor. Fossil footprints show that the ankylosaurs walked with their legs tucked well under their bodies. And muscle marks on the leg bones show that they could probably crouch down on the ground, to protect their soft underparts.

Nodosaurus

Borrowed head
Nodosaurus was over 16½ feet (5m) long and weighed up to 2 tons. It lived 90 million years ago in what is now the U.S. Body bones have been found, but no skulls. So scientists give it the head of a relative, *Panoplosaurus.*

Lumpy lizard
The name *Nodosaurus* means "lumpy lizard." Its armor was in the form of bony bumps in neat rows, large bumps alternating with small ones. This gave good protection yet could also bend easily as the creature moved about.

Hugging the ground
Study of the joints and muscle attachments of *Nodosaurus* reveals that it could probably "sit down," leaving only its armor exposed. An attacker would find it difficult to tip over, because of its great weight.

Long and strong
Nodosaurus's back legs were longer than the front ones, tipping its head down near the ground. The long back legs show how ankylosaurs had changed from the early bird-hipped dinosaurs, which walked on two legs only.

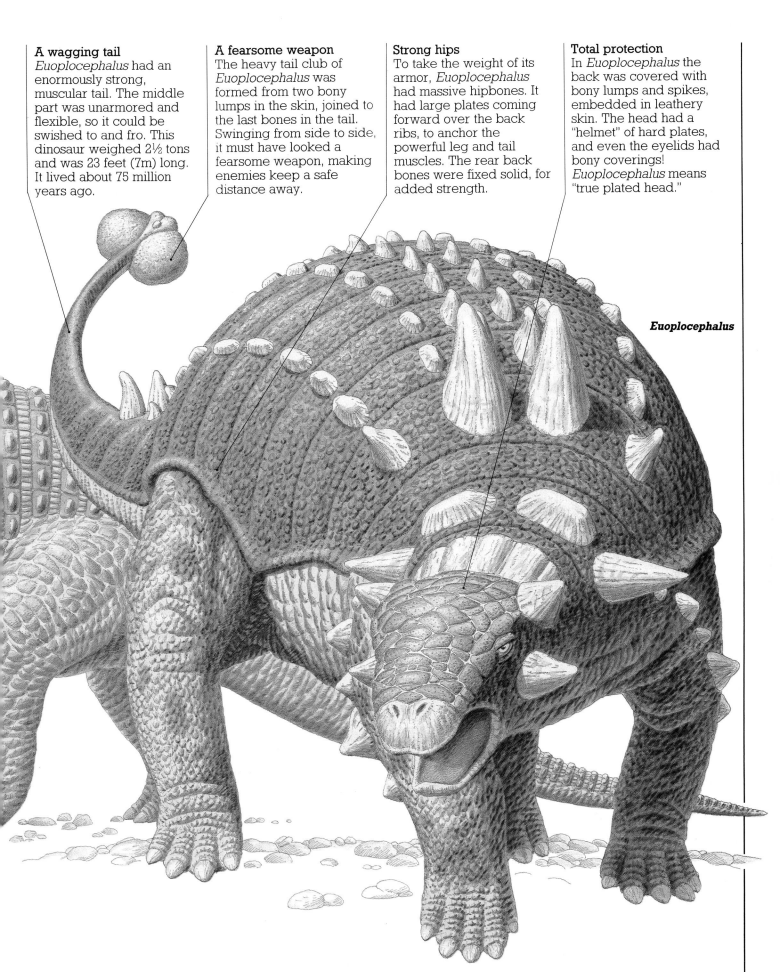

A wagging tail
Euoplocephalus had an enormously strong, muscular tail. The middle part was unarmored and flexible, so it could be swished to and fro. This dinosaur weighed 2½ tons and was 23 feet (7m) long. It lived about 75 million years ago.

A fearsome weapon
The heavy tail club of *Euoplocephalus* was formed from two bony lumps in the skin, joined to the last bones in the tail. Swinging from side to side, it must have looked a fearsome weapon, making enemies keep a safe distance away.

Strong hips
To take the weight of its armor, *Euoplocephalus* had massive hipbones. It had large plates coming forward over the back ribs, to anchor the powerful leg and tail muscles. The rear back bones were fixed solid, for added strength.

Total protection
In *Euoplocephalus* the back was covered with bony lumps and spikes, embedded in leathery skin. The head had a "helmet" of hard plates, and even the eyelids had bony coverings! *Euoplocephalus* means "true plated head."

Euoplocephalus

STEGOSAURUS

When fossils of *Stegosaurus* were first found, experts thought that its large bony plates lay flat on its back, like tiles on a roof. This is why its name means "roofed lizard." Then it was suggested that the plates stood on edge in a row – or perhaps in two rows, side by side. Yet more evidence now shows that one row of plates was probably slightly in front of the other, instead of them being side by side. This is what most experts believe today. People also used to think that *Stegosaurus* had two "brains," a tiny one in its head and a much larger one in the base of its tail, but this was not true. The spaces in the tail bones do show that the nerves inside were thicker than normal, but they probably just acted as a kind of "junction box" to help control the back legs and tail of the animal.

Slow and heavy
At 23 feet (7m) and weighing 1½ tons, Stegosaurus was almost certainly slow and lumbering. It lived 150 million years ago.

A brain as big as a nut
Stegosaurus probably had the smallest brain of any dinosaur. It was less than 2 inches (5cm) long – the size of a walnut. Experts are still puzzled by how these huge but small-brained animals survived for over 10 million years. Maybe *Stegosaurus* was stupid, but at that time cleverness was not very important. Whatever the reason, its brain was big enough for its needs.

A weak beak
Stegosaurus had leaf-shaped teeth at the back of its mouth but only a toothless "beak" at the front. It also had weak jaw muscles. So it could probably chomp only soft plants for food.

Straight or bent?
Stegosaurus's front legs were short, bringing its head near the ground for grazing. But were they straight or bent? Experts are not sure.

What were the plates for?

Why did *Stegosaurus* have such odd plates along its back? They were not sharply pointed for defense. They were not even fixed to the skeleton, but simply stuck in the skin. The best explanation is that they helped to control body temperature. The plates were honeycombed with holes, perhaps for blood vessels. When facing the sun, the plates would absorb heat (like solar panels) and warm the blood. When facing the breeze, the plates would cool.

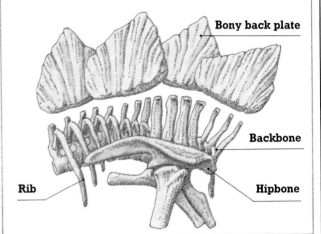

Bony back plate

Backbone

Rib

Hipbone

The largest plates

Stegosaurus was one of several dinosaurs, called stegosaurids, that had upright bony plates along their backs. *Stegosaurus* itself had the largest plates, some 30 inches (75cm) long. All the stegosaurs were bird-hipped dinosaurs.

Stiff with muscles

The tail was so muscle-bound and powerful that it was not very flexible. The last two pairs of bony plates were shaped like spikes 3 feet (1m) long. They could not be swung about much, but maybe their appearance scared off enemies.

Feet like an elephant

Stegosaurus had strong back legs, which were nearly twice as long as its front legs. Its flat feet had three big toes and one tiny one, designed for carrying weight and not for speed.

Stegosaurus

CURIOUS HEADS

The first four dinosaurs below are hadrosaurs, famous for their strangely-shaped heads. Their lumps, bumps, crests, and spines are made of thin bone, mostly hollow and connected to the air spaces in the nose. What were these odd shapes for? There are many ideas. Were they "snorkels" for swimming or wading in water with nearly all the body submerged? Doubtful, since no holes have been found in the ends of the crests. Were they "air tanks" to hold spare air while the dinosaur swam

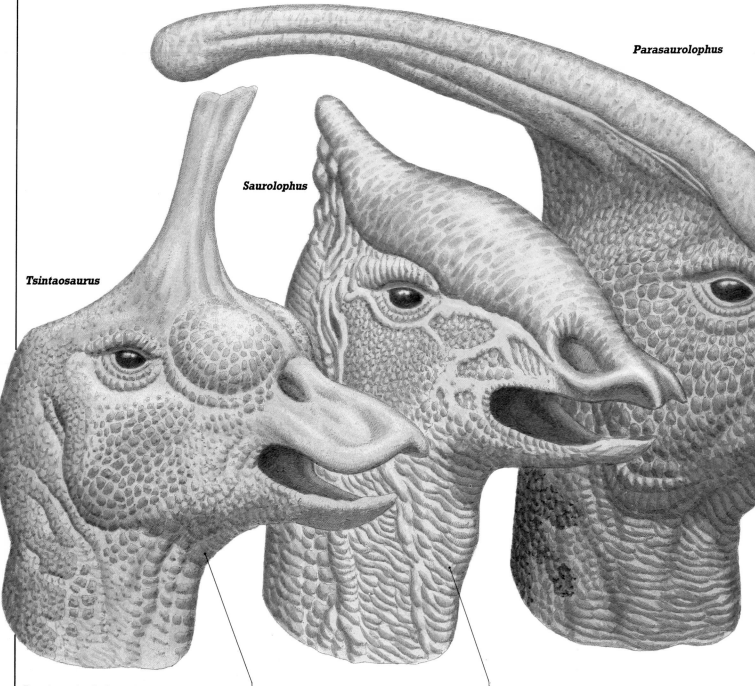

Parasaurolophus

Saurolophus

Tsintaosaurus

Putting their heads together
Hadrosaurs were relatives of Iguanodon, walking on back legs and eating plants. They were 23 to 33 feet (7-10m) long and lived about 70 million years ago. Despite their different-shaped heads they all had the same-shaped body.

Dinosaur unicorn
Tsintaosaurus, from China, had a hollow horn on its forehead (the only hadrosaur in which this points forward). Its fossil bones show that it may have had a balloonlike flap of skin over its nose. This could have been blown up to act as a "flag" signal or to make its call even louder.

The "ridged lizard"
The skull crest of *Saurolophus* was not hollow as in the other hadrosaurs. But, like its relatives, it had big eyes for a dinosaur. Also, fossil ear bones have been found for some hadrosaurs. This adds weight to the idea that the head crests were used for signaling by sight and sound.

42

underwater? Unlikely, since the space inside is too small for such a large creature. How about highly sensitive "nose extensions" for smelling, or "shields" to brush aside branches while running through undergrowth? Possibly, but this would not explain the variety of crest shapes and sizes.

Another explanation is that the head shapes acted as signals to other dinosaurs. Perhaps the crests were brightly colored, and waving the head meant "Keep away" or "I'm friendly." Possibly the hollow crest was a "resonator," vibrating to make the dinosaur's calls louder.

Corythosaurus

Pachycephalosaurus

Streamlined spike
Parasaurolophus had a long, thin, back-pointing crest, fitting into a notch in the backbone at the shoulder. In some cases it was as tall as an adult human! It could have been used to push aside branches. Some fossil skulls have smaller crests. These may be of females or young.

Head down, and run
The dinnerplate-shaped crest of *Corythosaurus* is similar to the crest of the cassowary, a flightless bird of today. The cassowary lives in forests in New Guinea and Australia, and it uses its head like a wedge to drive a path through thick undergrowth. Maybe this dinosaur did the same.

A spot of head-banging
Pachycephalosaurus had a strange head but it was not a hadrosaur. It belonged to another group, nicknamed "boneheads." The top of its skull bone was over 10 inches (25cm) thick. Perhaps there were head-butting contests at mating time, like sheep and goats have today.

43

THE STORY IN A SKULL

A fossil skull gives us lots of clues about the original creature. Many of the important parts of an animal are in and on its head – eyes, ears, and nose for finding out about the surroundings; jaws, teeth, and tongue for taking in food; brain for controlling the body; nose and mouth for breathing; spikes and armor for protection, and so on.

All dinosaur skulls are built on the same basic plan, with hollows for the eyes, a space inside for the brain, channels and holes for nerves and blood

vessels, and marks showing where the muscles for the jaws, tongue, and face were attached. By comparing skulls from other dinosaurs, and from reptiles and other animals alive today, we can make some good guesses about what a skull's owner looked like. Here are two very different dinosaur skulls. *Edmontosaurus*, as its name suggests, was dug up near Edmonton in Canada (*its hadrosaur cousins are on page 42*). Fossils of the carnosaur *Allosaurus*, "strange reptile," are from the U.S.

Leaves for lunch
Edmontosaurus *was the largest of the "duck-billed" dinosaurs, from the hadrosaur group. Nearly 43 feet (13m) long and 3 tons in weight, it was probably a slow mover with few defenses.*

Shape of the brain
In some *Edmontosaurus* fossils, mud has filled the space inside the skull and then turned to rock. This gives us a ready-made "cast" of the brain shape. The parts dealing with sight, hearing, and smell were well developed, indicating sharp senses.

Wide-eyed look
The large eye sockets suggest that *Edmontosaurus* had eyes perhaps 4 inches (10cm) across, giving a wide view. A large opening in the skull for the optic nerve (from eye to brain) is also evidence of good eyesight.

Teeth and tongue in cheek
Fossilized stomach remains show that some hadrosaurs ate tough, woody plant material like twigs and pine needles. *Edmontosaurus* had a thousand teeth cemented into large chewing pads at the back of its mouth. Hollows above and below the teeth show that the dinosaur may have had strong cheek pouches, like some present-day animals.

A crying dinosaur?
Some plants contain a lot of salt. Many modern reptiles and birds have "salt glands" near their eyes that get rid of the extra salt, as salty "teardrops." *Edmontosaurus* had hollows in the bones in front of its eyes, where salt glands may have been.

Blowing its nose
The shape of the front of the skull suggests that *Edmontosaurus* had loose skin on its nose, which it could blow up like a balloon. If the skin was brightly colored it might have been used to communicate with other dinosaurs in the herd.

A meaty meal
150 million years ago the fearsome meat-eater Allosaurus *preyed on creatures like* Edmontosaurus. *Almost 40 feet (12m) long, it had a giant skull in relation to its body – nearly 3 feet (1m) long.*

Sharp-eyed hunter
Allosaurus had large eyes, nearly twice the size of those of the much bigger meat-eater *Tyrannosaurus*. Above the eye was a bony flap forming an eyebrow ridge – possibly to shade its eyes from the sun.

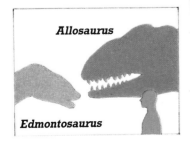

Fierce teeth
Allosaurus had about 40 teeth in its upper jaw and 32 in the lower jaw. They were up to 4 inches (10cm) long and their front and back edges were sharp and serrated, like steak knives, for slicing through flesh. The teeth pointed back into the mouth, to prevent the food from slipping out. As they wore out or broke, new teeth grew in their place.

Open wide . . .
Normally, the separate skull bones are joined very firmly (except for the jaws). Several joints in the skull of *Allosaurus* were loose and floppy. So this hunter could "bend" its mouth and open it extra wide to gulp down huge chunks of meat.

45

MOTHER AND BABIES

Laying eggs with shells was one of the reasons that reptiles, including the dinosaurs, became so successful. The amphibians before them could live on land, but they had to return to ponds and lakes to lay their jelly-coated eggs, which hatched into tadpoles (today's amphibians do the same). A reptile egg, however, has a tough, waterproof shell. Inside, the baby has its own watery "pond" in which to develop and grow. An egg with a hard shell meant that reptiles could spend all their time on land. The shell has another "advantage" – it is hard enough to fossilize. Since 1978 some exciting discoveries have been made about dinosaur eggs, in Montana. Fossils were found of eggshells, baby dinosaurs, and the nests they lived in. They belonged to a hadrosaur-type dinosaur that has been named *Maiasaura*, meaning "good mother lizard." These remains have given us some clues, not only about nests and babies, but also about how dinosaurs lived in general.

A dinosaur is born
A mother Maiasaura *looks on as her eggs hatch in their warm sandy nest, about 80 million years ago. Each pear-shaped egg is about 8 inches (20cm) long. The hatchlings are about 14 inches (35cm) long.*

Born in a bowl
The Montana finds include 15 fossilized young *Maiasaura* in and around a mound about 6½ feet (2m) across. Probably the mother scraped sand into a pile with her legs and scooped out the middle to a depth of about 3 feet (1m), for the eggs.

The dinosaur nursery
Several nests were found in a group. They were about 23 feet (7m) apart – the length of an adult *Maiasaura*. So these dinosaurs probably nested in colonies. This way, one or two parents would always be around to ward off predators.

A large family
There were 20 or more eggs in each nest, partly covered by sand. Perhaps the parent covered or uncovered the eggs according to the heat of the sun, so that they would incubate properly.

Staying at home
Experts think that the babies probably stayed in or near the nest for some time. Remains of older youngsters have been found near the mounds. Their teeth were worn by eating, so maybe their parent brought food back to the nest for them.

Also, the eggshells were broken into pieces, presumably by the young moving around. In other cases, such as that of *Hypsilophodon* eggs, the eggshells are in a few large pieces. These dinosaurs probably left the nest immediately after they had hatched out.

Dinosaur orphans?
Some nests have been found with fossilized babies in them. It may be that the *Maiasaura* parents were killed. The instincts of the young would tell them to stay in the nest, whatever happened.

47

BIG EATERS

Tyrannosaurus, the "tyrant lizard," is probably the most famous meat-eating dinosaur of all. Its fossils were first dug up in Montana in 1902. In the forests of 70 million years ago it must have ruled supreme, with its powerful body and legs and its frightening 6-inch (15-cm) teeth. In complete contrast is the enormous *Mamenchisaurus*, a sauropod from China. Its tiny head, long neck, fat body and bulky tail made it look slow and bulky – a mountain of flesh waiting to be pounced on by hunters like *Tyrannosaurus*.

These two creatures represent two very different types of dinosaurs, and it is tempting to think that the hunters were always superior to those they hunted, attacking them with ease whenever they wanted. Yet both these types of dinosaurs lived for millions of years. Meat-eaters could not have had it all their own way: if they had become too successful, they would have run out of food! It would seem that in the world of dinosaurs, as in the natural world today, nature kept a balance between the hunters and the hunted.

The long and the tall
Mamenchisaurus *has the typical shape of a giant plant-eater, with a small head and bulbous body.* Tyrannosaurus *looks every inch a powerful hunter.*

Holding its tail out
Tyrannosaurus is often shown in pictures with a long tail dragging on the ground. In fact no complete fossils of its tail bones have ever been found. It is more likely that *Tyrannosaurus* held its tail out straight, in order to counterbalance its head.

Infrequent eater
As we know from studying animals living today, big meat-eating reptiles do not need to kill and eat several times each day. The flesh on a medium-sized dinosaur carcass may have kept *Tyrannosaurus* going for weeks, even months.

Body posture
Past reconstructions of *Tyrannosaurus* usually show its body quite upright and its tail curled round. But it is more likely that the body was held horizontal, to help it keep its balance.

No doubt about size
The sheer size of *Tyrannosaurus* has never been in doubt. It grew up to 46 feet (14m) in length, its head was 16½ feet (5m) off the ground, and it may have weighed up to 7 tons.

Not so fast!
Tyrannosaurus had powerful legs. But, because of its size, it is doubtful that it could run at speed for long. Fossilized footprints show that it probably walked about as fast as a human, 2 or 3 miles (4-5km) per hour.

The longest neck

Mamenchisaurus lived about 140 million years ago. It is named after the place in China where its fossils were discovered in 1952. At 72 feet (22m), it is almost as long as its cousin *Diplodocus*. Indeed its neck, at 33 feet (10m), is even longer than the neck of *Diplodocus*. Although the neck looks flexible it could bend only a little, swinging from side to side as the dinosaur raked up plant food. Chinese museum-goers are probably as familiar with the fossils of this dinosaur as Americans are with the skeletons of *Diplodocus*.

Tiny hands

It is not clear what *Tyrannosaurus* used its tiny hands for. Good fossils of the fingers have not been found, so a two-clawed hand is based on that of a relative, *Albertosaurus*.

Dead or alive?

Tyrannosaurus certainly had a massive skull and powerful jaws. Its teeth were long and incredibly sharp, with serrated edges like steak knives. This "hunter" might, however, have been more of a scavenger, picking on dying animals or dead ones (carrion) for food.

"TERRIBLE CLAW"

In 1964 in Montana, a new kind of dinosaur was discovered. Many fossilized bones were found, enough to make several almost complete skeletons, in a dinosaur "graveyard" about 110 million years old. The newcomer was a lizard-hipped dinosaur belonging to the theropod group (*see page 16*), along with *Tyrannosaurus* and the "ostrich dinosaurs." It was around 5 feet (1.5m) tall and about 10 feet (3m) long. Lightly built, it weighed about 170 pounds (75-80kg) at the most – roughly the same size as an adult man. But the most startling thing about this new dinosaur was the long, thin, curved claw on the second toe of each foot. The newcomer was given the name of *Deinonychus*, which means "terrible claw."

The discovery of *Deinonychus* set the experts thinking. At the time, most people looked upon dinosaurs as slow, clumsy and stupid creatures. But the fossils of *Deinonychus* show that it was probably just the opposite – a quick, agile and clever creature. It must have been a busy hunter, with sharp senses. Some experts think that *Deinonychus* could have lived the way of life indicated by its fossils only if it was warm-blooded. (*You can read more about this on pages 54-55.*)

Predator on the run
Running at full speed on its powerful back legs, its fearsome toe claws at the ready, Deinonychus *tries to turn a smaller* Hypsilophodon *into a meal.*

Stiffened for steering
The tail was flexible at the base, where it joined the body. But along most of its length the back bones were stiffened by long, bony rods that could lock the tail straight. The tail acted as a counterbalance when running, and might have been swung to the side to help steer around corners when running at speed or when kicking.

Claws that could kill

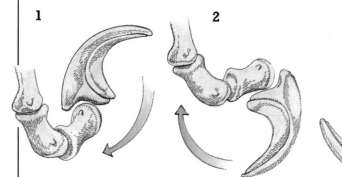

1   2   3

The main claw bone on each foot of *Deinonychus* was almost 5 inches (12cm) long, thin and curved like a sickle. It would have been covered by a horny sheath, like a nail. When not being used it was probably held up out of the way (**1**) to keep it razor-sharp. On the attack, *Deinonychus* would have kicked out strongly. To make the claw even more dangerous it could be swung downward on its toe (**2** and **3**) to slice long slits in the prey.

Light-headed dinosaur

The skull bones of *Deinonychus* show that it had a big brain and large eyes. Presumably it was an alert and cunning hunter. The skull itself was not solid bone, but had many large "windows" in it, through which muscles for the jaws and other parts passed. This made it very light.

High-kicking back legs

The leg bones and joints, and the scars on the bones where the muscles were attached, show that *Deinonychus* could kick out strongly as it slashed with its claw. It probably kicked with one leg, balancing on the other leg with the help of its tail. No modern reptile is so agile.

Snap shut and hang on

Deinonychus had more than 70 long, sharp, backward-pointing teeth. The muscles that held the jaws shut were especially large. Once this dinosaur had disabled its prey with its toe claws, it may have snapped its jaws shut, then hung on until it tore away a mouthful of flesh.

Deinonychus was 10 to 11½ feet (3-3.5m) long.

A deadly embrace

The arm bones are long and strong and they suggest that the arms and wrists could be twisted. Perhaps *Deinonychus* threw its arms around its prey and then held on as it stabbed with its feet. The three sharp, curved claws on each hand are more evidence for this idea.

ON THE ATTACK

Deinonychus lived at the same time as large plant-eating dinosaurs such as ankylosaurs, Iguanodon and Tenontosaurus. Yet Deinonychus was quite small. It would have had trouble tackling an animal as big as Iguanodon, which itself lived in herds. However, today's predatory creatures give us some clues. Many large meat-eaters, such as wolves, live in packs. They hunt together, several members attacking the same victim. In the case of prey that live in herds, they single out an old, young, or sick animal. In this way they improve their chances of a kill. It is likely that Deinonychus also hunted in packs like this.

Victim of the claw
Bird-hipped Tenontosaurus lived 110 million years ago. It was closely related to Hypsilophodon (see page 28). About 20 feet (6m) long, it weighed up to 1 ton – ten times as much as Deinonychus.

Going for the belly
The Deinonychus pack probably attacked the soft underside of their prey. For an armored dinosaur, like an ankylosaur, they may have tried to flip it over. Only a young ankylosaur could be turned over like this.

Not easy meat
Tenontosaurus was probably not an easy catch. It was an alert and powerful creature, moving swiftly on its long, strong legs. The thick, well-muscled tail could be swung at attackers to "slap" them away.

The pack principle – strength in numbers
A Deinonychus pack has caught a large, slow-moving Tenontosaurus. Some of the pack slash out with their sharp toe claws, while others bite and tear with their teeth. Soon the Tenontosaurus, already weak from its wounds, will be dead and eaten.

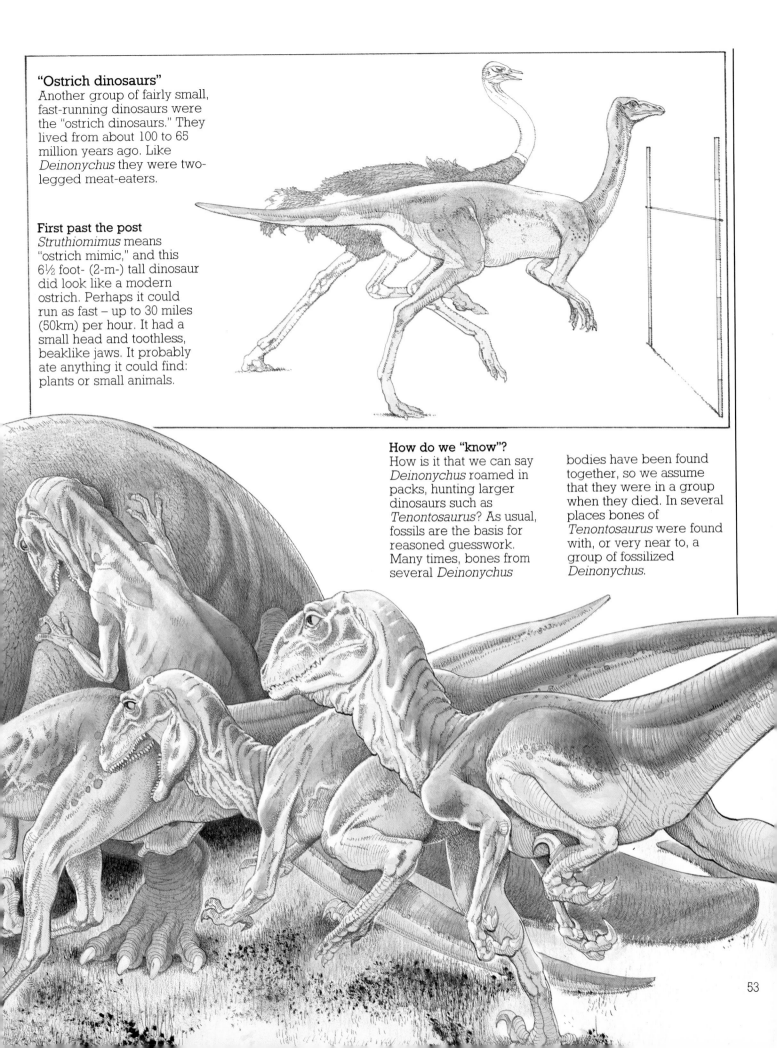

"Ostrich dinosaurs"

Another group of fairly small, fast-running dinosaurs were the "ostrich dinosaurs." They lived from about 100 to 65 million years ago. Like *Deinonychus* they were two-legged meat-eaters.

First past the post

Struthiomimus means "ostrich mimic," and this 6½ foot- (2-m-) tall dinosaur did look like a modern ostrich. Perhaps it could run as fast – up to 30 miles (50km) per hour. It had a small head and toothless, beaklike jaws. It probably ate anything it could find: plants or small animals.

How do we "know"?

How is it that we can say *Deinonychus* roamed in packs, hunting larger dinosaurs such as *Tenontosaurus*? As usual, fossils are the basis for reasoned guesswork. Many times, bones from several *Deinonychus* bodies have been found together, so we assume that they were in a group when they died. In several places bones of *Tenontosaurus* were found with, or very near to, a group of fossilized *Deinonychus*.

WARM-HEARTED DINOSAURS?

Were dinosaurs cold- or warm-blooded? For many years it was assumed that, like reptiles today, they were cold-blooded. Recently this traditional view has been challenged. First, though, what exactly do we mean by "cold" and "warm" blood?

"Warm-blooded" creatures – mammals and birds – keep their body temperature high (around 95-100°F, or 35-40°C). This is usually well above the temperature of their surroundings, and it is kept constant by chemically "burning" food to generate heat. Staying warm means an animal's body works more efficiently and it can keep active, looking for food and shelter whatever the conditions. Fur or feathers help to keep warmth in. However, a warm-blooded animal needs a lot of food.

"Cold-blooded" creatures like reptiles need less food, perhaps only one-tenth the amount a warm-blooded animal needs. But they are more at the mercy of their surroundings. If they soak up heat from the sun or warm rocks, their temperature rises and they can be active. When it is cold, at night or in the winter, their body temperature falls and so they are inactive.

What about the dinosaurs? Mammals and birds are numerous today, and they are warm-blooded. Were dinosaurs, which ruled for so long, warm-blooded too? Was that the secret of their success? Here are some of the arguments for and against their being warm-blooded.

Body size and design
Size and shape affect the "warm-blooded" discussion. Compare Dromiceiomimus, *an "ostrich dinosaur" from 70 million years ago, with the sauropod* Saltasaurus.

Busy means energy
Dromiceiomimus looks like a quick, active creature. It probably raced about on its back legs, alert and wide-eyed, escaping from bigger dinosaurs and chasing after small prey. It is difficult to imagine a cold-blooded animal keeping up this level of activity.

Bones under the microscope
The microscopic structure of fossil dinosaur bones is more similar to mammals than to living reptiles. But a bone's structure depends on the weight of the animal it supports and on how fast the bone grows. So this evidence is not clear.

Saltasaurus

Dromiceiomimus

Big-hearted reptile

A big dinosaur like *Saltasaurus* must have had a very strong heart, to pump blood many feet up to its head. But what if its heart was the same design as today's reptiles, pumping the same blood to the head, body, and lungs? The power of the heart pumping blood up the neck would make the blood pressure so high that it would damage the delicate blood vessels in the lungs. Perhaps its heart was more like a mammal's, divided into two parts, one for the lungs and the other for the head, body, and legs. This could mean it was warm-blooded.

Keeping the brain warm

Some dinosaurs had quite big brains. A large brain is very delicate and needs a constant temperature plus a plentiful blood supply in order to work efficiently. Warm-bloodedness would satisfy these needs better than the cold-blooded version.

Keeping cool – or warm

Some dinosaurs, such as *Stegosaurus* (*see page 40*), had plates, fins, or sails on their backs. These may have helped the creature warm up quickly when cold, and then cool down before getting too hot – so keeping its body temperature fairly regular.

Will we ever know?

It is doubtful we'll ever know for sure whether dinosaurs were warm-blooded. Maybe some were. However, the discussion is very useful, helping to increase our knowledge and understanding.

Bigger animals stay warmer

Large objects (including animals) lose heat more slowly than small ones. Perhaps this is why some dinosaurs came to be so big. They would soak up heat from the sun during the day, and then cool down slowly at night.

55

BIRDS OF A FEATHER

What is a bird? The main feature of a bird is that it has feathers. *Archaeopteryx* is a famous fossil creature from 150 million years ago, and its remains show that it had feathers. So it must have been a bird. Yet it also had many features of reptiles, and at least 20 features in common with small dinosaurs called coelurosaurs. Experts still argue about whether *Archaeopteryx* was a feathered dinosaur, or the first bird, or something in between. Some people believe it evolved from an earlier group of reptiles, and not from the dinosaurs. It wasn't even a true "in between" with a body that was gradually evolving from reptile to bird. Some parts of *Archaeopteryx* were just like a reptile's and others were like a modern bird's! *Archaeopteryx* is also

involved in the discussion as to whether dinosaurs, and maybe other reptiles, were warm-blooded (*see page 54*). So what *is* known about *Archaeopteryx*? It was the size of a crow. It had a large brain, big eyes, feathers, and a wishbone, like today's birds. Its feathers may have developed originally from reptile scales that did not grow properly, but their fluffiness helped to keep the creature warm. Only later did its winglike front limbs become strong enough for the feathers to be useful in flying.

Could *Archaeopteryx* fly?

Fossilized feathers

There are five known fossils of *Archaeopteryx*, or "ancient wing," all found in German limestone rocks. The first was dug up in 1855 but thought to be a pterosaur. It wasn't recognized as *Archaeopteryx* until 1973! The next find was in 1861 in a quarry. The fine grains of the limestone preserved the tiniest details, even feathers. The fossil shown here was discovered in 1877 and is kept in the Museum of Natural History in East Berlin. Unlike the other fossils found, it shows *Archaeopteryx*'s head and neck clearly.

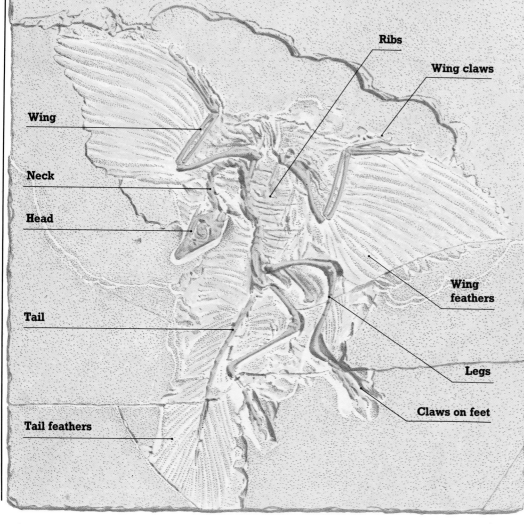

Ribs

Wing claws

Wing

Neck

Head

Tail

Wing feathers

Legs

Claws on feet

Tail feathers

It is doubtful that *Archaeopteryx* could really fly. Its skeleton and wing muscles were not strong enough for flapping flight. It may have clambered into tree branches and then jumped, gliding to another tree or to the ground. Or perhaps it ran fast along the ground after food, jumping, flapping its wings, and gliding.

Flying after flies
Why did birds start flying? Perhaps Archaeopteryx ran and jumped after insect food such as flies, as shown here. Any help in staying airborne, such as waving its feathered "arms," would be an advantage, and help it to survive.

Reptile teeth, bird brain
Like many reptiles, *Archaeopteryx* had teeth in its mouth. No modern bird has teeth in its beak. However, its big brain and large eyes were birdlike and not at all reptilian.

Claws for climbing
Each wing had three separate fingers with claws on the end. Although this is not quite like a modern bird, it is very different from the wing of a flying reptile like a pterosaur (*see pages 30-31*). Only one bird today has a wing claw – the young of the hoatzin from South America. Perhaps *Archaeopteryx*, like the baby hoatzin, used its claws for clambering about in trees.

Bones in the tail
In a modern bird there are no bones in the tail. Its shape is made entirely of feathers. *Archaeopteryx* had a bony tail, like a reptile, but with feathers down each side. It could have been used to help *Archaeopteryx* steer, as it flapped and glided along.

Feet for perching
The scales on the legs and feet of modern birds suggest a link with reptiles in the past. *Archaeopteryx* had scales here too. Of its four toes, the first one pointed backward, so that the foot could grip a branch and perch exactly like a bird of today.

Not a bird's bones
Archaeopteryx's bones were not light, its backbone was not stiff, and its breastbone did not have a "keel" on it. A modern bird has all these features, to make its skeleton stronger where the powerful wing-flapping muscles are anchored to it.

THE END OF THE DINOSAURS

Perhaps the greatest dinosaur mystery of all is: why did they die out? About 64 or 65 million years ago all the dinosaurs disappeared over a comparatively short period of time. Why? There have been many theories, but none of them fits all the fossil evidence. Another puzzle is that many other creatures died out at the same time as the dinosaurs, including sea-dwelling reptiles, pterosaurs, and ammonites. Also, this extinction was not the only one in our planet's past. Three-quarters of amphibians, for example, disappeared just before the appearance of the dinosaurs. We may never know what caused these extinctions.

The great catastrophe

According to one theory, the dinosaurs and other creatures perished because of a great disaster which affected the whole world. Perhaps the Earth was cloaked in dust as it passed through a swarm of comets or the debris from an exploding star. Many people think it might even have been hit by a giant meteorite.

1 The meteorite strikes

Scientists have discovered a layer of rock 65 million years old that contains much iridium – a substance rare on our planet but common in meteorites. Maybe a giant meteorite, 6 miles (10km) across, crashed into Earth.

2 Blotting out the sun

Dust thrown up by the meteorite would have blotted out the sun for years. Plants would not have been able to grow, and plant-eating animals would have starved. Many animals would have frozen to death.

3 From cold to hot

As the dust settled, water vapor thrown up by the meteorite would have trapped heat as the sun gradually broke through, making the Earth warmer. Many animals might now have died from the heat.

Out with a whimper?

It is difficult to tell from fossils whether the dinosaurs died out over a few dozen years or over a million years. Several theories about their extinction are based on the idea that the dinosaurs died out gradually over a long period of time without a sudden worldwide catastrophe.

A change in the weather?
Some experts suggest that rocks and fossils show the world's climate was changing 65 million years ago. Year-round tropical warmth gave way to a seasonal climate, with hot summers and cool winters. If the dinosaurs were cold-blooded they might not have been able to cope with these variations.

Poisoned by plants?
Many dinosaurs were plant-eaters. Possibly the new kinds of flowering plants that appeared were poisonous to the dinosaurs (and any other creatures that ate them). As the plant-eaters died, the flesh-eating dinosaurs, which relied on the plant-eaters for food, would also have slowly starved to death.

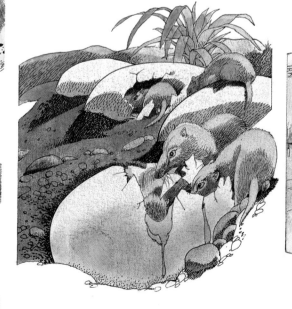

Did the egg-stealers win?
Many creatures, such as mammals and birds, eat the eggs of today's reptiles. Could it be that the small mammals of 65 million years ago became too good at stealing and eating dinosaur eggs? They would have been active at night, when any dinosaur "parents" would have been too cold and slow to stop them.

Changing habitats
During the last few million years of the Age of Dinosaurs, sea levels dropped all around the world and more land appeared, as mountains rose from the plains. The shallow seas that had covered vast areas of most of the continents dried up and creatures that lived around them, such as the dinosaurs, lost their habitats.

DINOSAUR DESCENDANTS?

The dinosaurs have all gone. But do they "live on" in some form – did they leave any descendants? Are any of today's creatures the "great-great-great-grandchildren" of the dinosaurs? Of the five big groups of backboned animals (fish, amphibians, reptiles, birds, and mammals), fish and amphibians had evolved well before the dinosaurs (*see pages 14-15*), so they cannot be their descendants. That leaves reptiles, birds, and mammals. Examining the fossil evidence, it may be that of all the different creatures crocodiles and birds are the closest living relatives of the dinosaurs.

Who is their closest relative?

When studying evolution and who is related to whom, you must examine the whole animal – not just look at its outward appearance. An armadillo may look like a dinosaur, but it isn't. It is a mammal, feeding its young on milk.

Mammals

Dinosaurs ruled the world 100 million years ago. Today, mammals do the same. Some mammals, like elephants and rhinoceroses, are big and have tusks shaped like some dinosaur horns. But there are several reasons why mammals cannot be descended from dinosaurs. Mammals are warm-blooded, have fur or hair, give birth to babies, and feed them on milk. Dinosaurs, being reptiles, were probably cold-blooded (*see page 54*) and had scaly skin. Fossils show that they laid eggs. So the two groups are quite different. Even more important, mammals already existed when the Age of Dinosaurs began. They were probably descended from the therapsids (mammal-like reptiles), while the dinosaurs probably evolved from reptiles called thecodonts.

Elephant

Rhinoceros

Armadillo

Reptiles

The dinosaurs were reptiles, so aren't their closest living relatives reptiles? Not necessarily! Reptiles were evolving nearly 300 million years ago. During the next 100 million years, they split into many different groups – including the ancestors of today's snakes and lizards, tortoises and turtles. So all these groups of reptiles already existed when the dinosaurs first appeared. The curious tuatara of New Zealand is the last member of another group of reptiles that appeared alongside the ancestors of lizards and early dinosaurs, around about 200 million years ago.

Birds

Did certain dinosaurs evolve into birds? Possibly. The bird hipbone is very like the hipbone of bird-hipped dinosaurs. The skeleton of *Archaeopteryx*, the first bird, is similar to that of small, early dinosaurs called coelurosaurs. The skulls of dinosaurs and fossil birds are also alike. They both have a hole in front of the eye socket – an important evolutionary feature. There are outward similarities, too. Birds like the emu and ostrich look similar to the "ostrich dinosaurs." Hoatzin chicks have wing claws like *Archaeopteryx* (*see page 56*).

Crocodiles

Fossil crocodiles had the important hole in the skull, just in front of the eye socket, like dinosaurs. And the crocodile's hipbone is similar to the hipbones of saurischian ("lizard-hipped") dinosaurs. All in all, birds and crocodiles are probably the closest living relatives of the dinosaurs.

Galapagos iguana

Turtle

Tuatara

Hoatzin

Emu

Crocodile

DINOSAUR PICTURE GALLERY

If you saw a dinosaur walking along your street, would you recognize it? Maybe you could check it off on our Picture Gallery. Although dinosaurs have been dead for 65 million years, some of them are more famous than many creatures still alive today. Here are some of the biggest, smallest, oddest, and scientifically most important dinosaurs. Have you seen them recently, in a museum or exhibition?

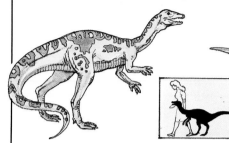

Coelophysis (See-low-fye-siss)
One of the first dinosaurs, from 200 million years ago, its fossils were first found in the U.S. It was a flesh-eating theropod (*see page 16*).

Compsognathus (Comp-sog-nay-thuss)
This dinosaur, whose fossils are 145 million years old, is one of the smallest ever found. It was a meat-eater (*see pages 26-27*).

Deinonychus (Dye-non-eye-kuss)
The famous "terrible claw" lived 110 million years ago. A lizard-hipped dinosaur, it was a fierce hunter (*see page 50*).

Baryonyx (Barry-on-icks)
This newcomer to the dinosaur hall of fame lived 120-odd million years ago and was a meat-eater. Its remains include a huge claw (*see page 28*).

Allosaurus (Al-owe-saw-russ)
A "carnosaur," a type of two-legged meat-eater, this creature of 150 million years ago was a well-equipped hunter (*see pages 44-45*).

Tyrannosaurus (Tie-ran-owe-saw-russ)
The "king of the dinosaurs," from 70 million years ago, walked on two legs and was the biggest flesh-eating land creature ever (*see page 48*).

Plateosaurus (Plat-ee-owe-saw-russ)
A very early dinosaur from 200 million years ago, this creature was one of the first big four-legged plant-eaters (*see page 16*).

Diplodocus (Dip-lod-o-kuss)
The longest dinosaur known to science, this lightly built plant-eater walked the Earth around 140 million years ago (*see page 24*).

Apatosaurus (A-pat-owe-saw-russ)
Another plant-eater that lived at the same time as *Diplodocus*, this "deceptive lizard" was once known as *Brontosaurus* (*see page 24*).

Brachiosaurus (Brack-ee-owe-saw-russ)
This giant is the most massive land creature known to science. It lived 140 million years ago and was one of the sauropods (*see page 24*).

Hypsilophodon (Hip-si-low-fo-don)
This small dinosaur roamed southeast England 120 million years ago. It was an ornithopod, a "bird-footed" dinosaur (*see page 28*).

Iguanodon (Ig-wahn-owe-don)
Like *Hypsilophodon*, this well-known dinosaur was a two-legged plant-eater. It lived around 120 million years ago (*see page 4*).

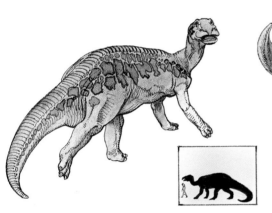

Edmontosaurus (Ed-mon-toe-saw-russ)
A hadrosaur, or "duck-billed," ornithischian, *Edmontosaurus* was a plant-eater. It lived 150 million years ago (*see page 44*).

Protoceratops (Proe-toe-serra-tops)
Fossils of this early horned dinosaur, 80 million years old, come from Mongolia and include remains of eggs (*see page 34*).

Triceratops (Try-serra-tops)
A ceratopian (horned dinosaur), this three-horned beast was a bird-hipped dinosaur and lived 65 million years ago (*see page 36*).

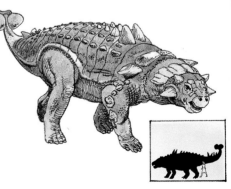

Pachycephalosaurus (Pack-ee-sef-allo-saw-russ)
This dinosaur was named "thick-headed lizard" because of its helmet-like skull (*see page 43*).

Stegosaurus (Steg-owe-saw-russ)
As big as an elephant, this bird-hipped dinosaur from 150 million years ago had one of the smallest brains of all (*see page 40*).

Euoplocephalus (You-owe-plo-sef-a-luss)
This well-protected ankylosaur (armored dinosaur) lived about 75 million years ago (*see page 39*).

INDEX